M. T.

"A View of Warsaw from Vistula", drawing by Bernardo Bellotto (Canaletto younger),
18th century

WARSAW

Photography: St. Jabłońska, K. Jabłoński and R. Jabłoński
Text: Jarosław Zieliński
Translation: Stanisław Semczuk

Warsaw 1994
Publisher FESTINA, Warszawa, tel. 42-54-53
ISBN 83-900-690-3-2

T he exact date of city foundation is not known. It is generally assumed that the city was founded soon after 1294 which was the starting year of the rule of Bolesław II, Duke of Mazovia an independent Dukedom with the capital in Płock. The city was set on a virgin ground though various settlements had been known around since the 10th century. These were Bródno, Ujazdów, Solec, Kamion and Warszowa. Warszowa, the property of Warsz Rawita, which occupied the area of the present Mariensztat lent the name to the Polish capital.

Another city known as Nowa Warszawa (New Warsaw) was located near Warsaw in about 1400. The custom of setting many towns at adjacent locations was quite popular in the medieval Europe.

Old Warsaw secured with multiple economic and government privileges developed quickly. A document of 1338 mentions the city walls and three churches: the parish church of St. John, Holy Spirit, and St. George. Probably only the first of them was a masonry structure. The document mentions also the "wójt" (sheriff's) house, later named incorrectly as the Dukes of Mazovia House, the structure rebuilt many times and preserved until today. The quoted document concerns the legal case of Poland v. The Teutonic Knights.

Mazovia was incorporated into Corona Regni Polnae after the extinction of Dukes of Mazovia in 1526. Old Warsaw was already a well developed city, while New Warsaw was about to remain for a long time a ramshackle suburb of her older sister. The relics of 15th and 16th century construction are visible in walls of the Royal Castle, portals and pieces of walls in the city houses as well as considerable pieces of the walls at the Bernardines Church in Krakowskie Przedmieście.

Profiting from its localisation in the centre of the country Warsaw became a residential city of the monarchs. 16th century was a very prosperous time for the burgers known for their wealth and education. The Sejm of Lublin of 1596 where the Republic (or Commonwealth) of the Two Nations (Poland and Lithuania) was established decided that all future Sejms would assemble at the Warsaw Castle. In 1576 the Royal Elections were transferred from Kraków. In 1596, the Wawel Castle in Krakow was destroyed by fire, provoking King Zygmunt III to move to Warsaw with the entire court.

The City ground proved to be too small in 15th century when the urban structure spilt over the double lines of the city walls and annexed the two suburbs: Czersk (Krakowskie Przedmieście now) and New Warsaw (Ul. Freta now). Warsaw housed 7 thousand citizens in 1564. Most of the buildings were gothic brick houses, though white plastered Renaissance became visible. The most spectacular investment of the time was the bridge over Vistula. The wooden structure was completed in 1573 and survived until the beginning of 17th century when it was destroyed by the flood. The Brama Mostowa (Bridge Gate) has been probably the last gothic styled structure built in Warsaw. Another cataclysm came in 1607 when the entire Old Warsaw burnt. The city was rebuilt very quickly though in a completely new, baroque and mannerists style. Some of the well preserved structures of that time are the houses "Pod Murzynkiem" and "Baryczkowska" in the northern side of the Old Town Market.

Ambitious burgers of 17 century copied the style of the new Royal buildings. Nonetheless the burgers estate shown visible symptoms of decay. The estate monarchy of Poland began to transform into the gentry's Republic where the grand land-owning families (the magnates) gathered political influence and ruled the country while the burgers were systematically weakened until the complete fall of the estate in 18th century.

Power of the Magnates has been epitomised by the palaces and mansions set usually at the edge of the Vistula vault scarp, along the present Krakowskie Przedmieście. These buildings erected in the first half of the 17th century were famous for their extravagance which overwhelmed not only Poles but the foreign visitors too. None of these structures exist in the original form though considerable relicts of these buildings have been preserved in the house of Caritas Society (Adam Kazanowski mansion), the Council of Ministers Palace (this belonged to Koniecpolski and later to the Radziwills) and "Dom pod Królami" (the palace of Daniłowicz). Another mark of the magnates' power were the so called "juridcs", i.e. private towns built around Old and New Warsaw to compete with the two Royal Cities. These towns were subject to separate law and were not submitted to the jurisdiction of the City authorities. At the end of 18 century there were as many as 20 "juridics" around Warsaw. Their names have been preserved as names of present streets, districts or suburbs: Leszno, Grzybów, Mariensztat, Kapitulna.

The crown was the most important investor. Royal residences in the city and in the country decided the fashion in construction. The major royal investments included new exterior of the Royal Castle, and the Ujazdów Castle (both restored to their 17th century shape). Relicts of another Vasa residence are hidden in the present buildings of the University known as "Pałac Kazimierzowski", after the King Jan Kazimierz of Vasa dynasty. Royal patronage enabled development of court arts, especially theatre and music.

The Swedish War of 1655-57 brought attacks by Swedish and Polish armies, total robbery by the Swedes and Transylvanians, destruction by fire of all the suburbs, epidemics and migration. The city was depopulated loosing 14 of 20 thousand citizens. Reconstruction took more than two decades and the former prosperity never returned.

Tylman van Cameren was the leading architect of the latter half of 17th century. His works include many mansions, palaces and churches, among them the famous Pałac Krasińskich rebuilt after the latest war only in the central part. Two churches are very interesting: the St. Boniface in Czerniaków with the authentic polychrome and stucco works preserved and St. Kazimir (Sacrament Sisters) in the New Town - built to commemorate king Jan III Sobieski victory over Turks on the outskirts of Vienna and funded by the Queen Maria Kazimiera. Sobieski built also Marywil, a commercial complex demolished at the beginning of 19th century when the Opera Theatre was constructed, as well as his residence in Wilanów, which retains a lot of its former shape despite refurbishments in 18th and 19th centuries.

The Northern War in the beginning of 18th century brought further destruction and depopulation. Surprisingly, the number of citizens doubled in 1720 which can be partly explained by migration from the war affected area.

The rule of Saxon Dynasty marks the beginning of the process which lead to loss of independence of the country whose candidates to throne were selected in Petersburgh. The magnates and the gentry reached the peak of their power in the country. Multiple mansions (for instance the mansions of Potocki and Czapski, now Ministry of Culture and Fine Arts Academy) and manor houses retaining a semi-rural character were added to the city landscape diminishing a few islands of strictly urban architecture. Still some burgers' houses had very high artistic value what is particularly clear with the houses of Leszczyński and Nowicki at Krakowskie Przedmieście 87/89. The sacral architecture was of course vital, the most interesting specimens being the Holy Cross and the close church of St.Joseph (Visiting Sisters). The latter is regarded as one of the greatest pieces of baroque architecture in Poland. Despite proverbial ignorance prevailing in the time first successful attempts to reform education structure had been taken then by Piar, Jesuit and Teatines orders. During the reign of the Saxon monarchs Warsaw enriched with the by then largest urban structure, the so called Saxon Axis modelled after Versailles. Warsaw streets were tidied by the Cobblestone Committee working under the vigorous leadership of marshal Franciszek Bieliński.

The last chapter in the history of the First Republic was marked by the reign of Stanisław August, an enlightened sponsor of arts but politically an impotent monarch in the weakened country completely dependent on Russia. Warsaw developed vigorously in that time. The population grew form 30 thousand in 1764 to 115 thousand in 1792. Jewish community of 6-7 thousand was the largest non Polish group in the town.

New buildings designed in fashionable classicist style appeared. The greatest new urban structure was Stanisław Axis, a system of star arranged plazas on the southern outskirts. The Żoliborz country-like suburb developed while a

9

typically industrial construction raised in Powiśle and Solec.

The jewel in the architecture of the time is the Łazienki Park, a complex of picturesque mansions and villas set in the park crossed with canals. Apart from the Pałac na Wodzie built as an island on a large pond, the most interesting object is the Orangery of wood only interior which housed the court theatre. Another important achievement of the time is a sequence of representative chambers and Royal Apartments in the Warsaw Castle. These latter were reconstructed in 1971 and they contain thousands of authentic pieces of décor and furnishing.

The great political event was adoption of the Constitution of May 3rd (1791). Modern Statutes guaranteed political rights to the burgers and abolished "juridics" providing the basis to modern development of the cities in the Republic.

Petersburgh reacted quickly to the dangerous political developements. The war of 1792 abolished the Constitution and gave power to the Targowica Society which was later joined by the broken King. The Kościuszko Uprising of April 1794 pushed the Russian Army out of the City and succeeded in defence against Prussian Army in September. Another attack of the Russians in November ended with the mass slaughter of the Praga suburb and capitulation of the terrorised city.

1795 is the year of definite extinction of the Polish State. The partition of the country left Warsaw within Prussia as a provincial, frontier, town. Loss of the political position resulted in depopulation (64829 people in 1798). The aristocracy left the town moving to their country residences. The Prussian rule continued until November 1806 when the French army entered the City. Napoleon created the so called Duchy of Warsaw, a minor political organism, but Warsaw became a capital city again. Constant wars, requisitions and contributions were typical for the Napoleon time. In addition to that the country had to support an unproportionally large army. In April 1809 Warsaw was shortly took over by the Austrians, though superior Polish regiments commanded by Prince Józef Poniatowski defeated them soon. The Moscow defeat of Napoleon in 1812 dramatically altered the fate of Warsaw. The Vienna Congress of 1815 created the Kingdom of Poland whose hereditary throne went to the Emperors of Russia. This way Poland had been attached to the Romanow dynasty for entire century.

The Kingdom of Poland which received from Emperor Alexander I liberal though often disobeyed statutes entered into a fifteen years long period of dynamic development. The state governed by bureaucracy and the police needed many buildings to house the administration. Old magnates' residences were often adapted after thorough refurbishment. A complex of Treasury and the National Bank has been preserved at the Plac Bankowy. The House of the Interior (Pałac Małachowskiego) in close vicinity former was designed as a

10

Government building by the leading architect of the time, Antonio Corrazzi. Profitable terms of crediting lead to construction of several hundreds of new houses, while urban planning enabled construction of streets and squares like Nowy Świat, Plac Teatralny or Plac Bankowy, which represented a homogeneous type of architecture. This was possible because the acceptance of all building plans lied in competence of the General Committee of Construction which corrected all transgressions. The most spectacular building of that time was the biggest Opera Theatre house in Europe, designed by Corrazzi.

In 1830 the city counted 140 thousand citizens. 30 thousand Warsaw Jews were moved to the north-west district in 1825. Despite that restrictions in settlement were latter abolished, this part of the city remained the Jewish community centre until the World War II. Nalewki, the high street of the district was demolished in 1943 together with the entire Getto.

Increasing limitations in the Kingdom independence and brutality of the Imperial Viceroys provoked considerable clandestine political activity and lead eventually to the outbreak of the anti-Russian uprising on November 19th 1830. The Polish Army together with armed civilians forced the Russian units to withdraw from the city and further from the Kingdom of Poland. The Sejm dethroned the Emperor Nicholas I form the Polish throne. In 1831 the war between The Kingdom and Russia began. In February the Polish Army managed to stop the Russian attacks at the Olszynka Grochowska on the outskirts of Warsaw. The forthcoming months brought a few successes which were eventually spoiled because of incompetence of the Polish high command. Warsaw was under siege again in September and capitulated after the attacks from the West. The defeat resulted in loss of independence, separate army, the Treasury and local government structures. The occupants began to size the Catholic churches and convert them into Orthodox ones. The major penalty though, was the construction of the Alexander Citadel which swallowed a large part of the Żoliborz suburb. The fortification enabled the Russians to keep the city under artillery fire in case of any disturbances. Further enlargement of this structure lead to new demolitions and stopped the development of the city into the North.

Post war repression stopped the development of the city for about ten years. The eighteen forties brought some economic grow which resulted mostly from abolition of the customs border with Russia in 1851. Metallurgy, chemical production and ceramics benefited the most. The industrial district moved from Powiśle to Wola and Praga. Industrial production in Warsaw employed about 7000 workers in 1862. Building boom of 1857-58 added 753 new "front" houses and 1033 "rear" ones. Considerable number of houses were heightened. Henryk Markoni was the leading architect of the time. Many of his designs were restored after the World War II, among them the Europejski Hotel at Krakowskie Przedmieście, the house of the Landowners Credit Company at

Plac Małachowskiego and the All Saints Church at Plac Grzybowski. In 1865 the city counted 236 thousand inhabitants and developed mostly into west and south. The most important investments of that time were railway (1845), water supply (1855), gas lights (1856) and paving of the streets.

Hardened politics of Russification provoked strong resistance. The demonstrations which ended with bloodshed and attempts of mass conscription to the Russian Army lead to the outbreak of the uprising of January 1863. In absence of the regular army the uprising was mostly a country guerrilla war which did not affect Warsaw. Warsaw was nonetheless the residence of the clandestine National Government. After the arrest and execution of Stanisław Traugutt, the last commander of the uprising, the hostilities gradually extinguished. The following reprisals brought the abolition of Polish schools, closure of the University and Fine Arts Academy. Abolition of the Building Committee enabled uncontrolled haphazard construction. The new law made all street and commercial signs double language.

The fortification belt built around the city was a real disaster because it hindered territorial expansion and squeezed building within the city borders. Although the restrictions in building outside fortifications were abolished in 1911 it brought little effect until the outbreak of the Great War. The density of urban structure is well illustrated when observed that while the area of the city grew twice between 1830 and 1914 the population grew 6 times (from 140 to 884 thousand). The houses were higher and often supplemented by another row if buildings in the back yard which lead to creation of characteristic, dim, well-like yards. Lack of building space affected even public houses often cramped on scraps of land between houses. Warsaw lacked parks and gardens having only 735 ft^2 of green area per person compared to 3033 ft^2 London had this time. Land reserves of the city were extinguished by building of more than 1300 houses and 3000 back yards attachments between 1868 and 1882 and further 4800 houses between 1891 and 1914. The most important constructions of the time were buildings of the Polytechnics, University Library, the house of Fine Arts Society (all designed by Stefan Szyller); the house of the Philharmonics by Karol Kozłowski (now completely refashioned), and Władysław Marconi designs of the Russian Insurance Company at Aleje Jerozolimskie 124 (refashioned completely after 1945), and Bristol Hotel at Krakowskie Przedmieście, restored recently to the former glory.

The buildings from the end of the century usually wore historical costume (neo-renaissance, neo-gothic, neo-classicism or neo-baroque) or were simply eclectic. Secession designs spread shortly after 1902 soon to be replaced by modern designs. All these fashions were visible best in the fronts of the apartment houses which, unlike the public buildings, could be constructed without Petersburgh approval. The remnants of this urban structure have been preserved along the streets: Aleje Jerozolimskie, Aleje Ujazdowskie and Foksal.

The most effective use of land and highest buildings can be seen at Plac Unii Lubelskiej, Polna and Noakowskiego. Lwowska is a rare example of the completely preserved street from this epoch. The most important early modern style were built between 1914 and 1917: the Bracia Jabłkowscy Department Store at Bracka 25 (by Karol Jankowski and Franciszek Lilpop) and the Bank pod Orłami at Jasna (by Jan Heurich).

Lack of urban infrastructure enforced construction of a new system of water supply and sewage. The contracts were given to British family of Lindley. The first bridge over Vistula was build 1864, two more were added until 1914. Among the latter was Most Poniatowskiego by Stefan Szyller, which preserved the neo-renaissance design until today. Telephones were introduced in the eighties while the first electric plant was built in 1903. This enabled introduction of electric street lights in 1907 and tramways in 1908. The latter replaced former horse driven tramways operating since 1865.

The revolution of 1905-06 in Warsaw was an anti-Russian uprising and brought a slight ease in Imperial rule in Poland enabling restitution of Polish schools and legalising a number of national societies.

The outbreak of the Great War in 1914 reversed the feelings of the population which supported the Russians against the Germans who entered Warsaw in 1915. The new occupation characterised with famine and requisitions. The Germans desperate for new conscripts created a nominally independent Kingdom of Poland. This semi-independence enabled quick development of local government and creation of rudiments of state administration. The borders of the city were eventually expanded by incorporation of the suburbs in the fortification belt. The new lands devoid of any infrastructure, consisted of haphazardly built wooden houses which made central Warsaw looking like an urban isle within a gigantic village.

On November 11th 1918 the German garrison had been disarmed by the civilians and some Polish units. This day is recognised as a day restoration of the country independence after 123 of foreign occupation. The Great War brought also decrease in city's population (758 400) mostly due to migration and epidemics.

The Polish-Soviet War of 1920 created a great threat to Poland and Europe. A series of battles on the outskirts of Warsaw lead to the defeat of the enemy by the recreated Polish Army.

First post war years marked by hyper-inflation did not encouraged new investment in the city. Nonetheless much was done to integrate the substandard suburbs. New housing districts in Żoliborz, Mokotów and Ochota developed until Word War II. Many individual owned houses and co-operative buildings were built. New school and public administration buildings were designed with considerable care.

The Great Economic Crisis stopped development of the city. Only after

13

Stefan Starzyński had been appointed the mayor, improvement in budget and development could be seen. Many ambitious projects were introduced to correct unplanned development of the turn of the century. Powiśle got a new boulevard, a street connecting the centre with Żoliborz was built and construction of the North-South avenue connecting Mokotów with Żoliborz began, though it had been completed only after the World War II. Some plans, like construction of the entire district on Pole Mokotwskie were forgotten after 1945. Great care was attached to restoration of the historical buildings and city's green areas. The architecture transformed adopting first the from the "country manor style" referring to Polish gentry manor house of 17th century visible in the Górnośląska street, then a moderate modernism visible in the Ministry of Education in Aleja Szucha and radical functionalism which can be seen in Warsaw co-operative houses in Żoliborz to finish with the luxurious designs of the late thirties (Jan Wedel house at Puławska, the streets of Przyjaciół and Juliana Bartoszewicza. The exhibition of Warsaw urban planning organised just before the World War II shown Warsaw as a modern city with many individual traits.

In 1939 Warsaw occupied 55 square miles (four times increase since 1915) while the population grew to 1289 thousand. The Jewish community counted about 300 thousand, a much lower number than in the twenties because of mass emigration to America and Palestine. The Jewish community traditionally dwelled the north-west part of the city and the western part of central Warsaw.

Nobody could foresee the results of the cataclysm which began on September 1st !939. Until September 27th, the day of capitulation of Warsaw, 12% of city structure had been ruined. Among these the most valuable historic monuments: the St. John Cathedral and the Royal Castle. The German plan of reprisals for the stubborn defence was the complete destruction and construction of a new small town for German settlers. Poles were about to settle in a camps at the right side of Vistula. New order began with the enforced resettlement of Jewish population to the north-west district which was surrounded by the wall. The Getto housed 400 thousand people, many brought from other towns. The remaining part was subject to man hunt (the victims were sent to the concentration camps or as a slave workforce to Germany) and mass executions. 300 thousand Warsawers died until August 1944. Soviet bombing of 1941-1943 caused little damage to the Germans but took a considerable death toll among the civilians.

The so called "liquidation" of the Warsaw Getto began in June 1942. During the following 50 days 300 thousand Warsaw Jews were transported to the gas chambers in Treblinka. The attempt to take the remaining few thousand lead to the outbreak of the uprising on April 19th 1943. Hopeless defence lasted until May 16th. Once the last nests of defence had been extinguished the Germans murderd all the remaining Jews and consequently demolished the area formerly occupied by the Getto.

The approaching Soviet army and the consequent threat of power seizure by the communists provoked the Home Army Command and the Polish Government in London to start the uprising in Warsaw. The overwhelming strength of the Germans and complete passivity of the Soviets lead to the defeat after 63 days of fighting. The death toll among the fighters and civilians reached 200 thousand. The rest of the population was expelled from the city which was later systematically demolished. The demolition affected also the most valuable historical monuments. Only on January 17th 1945 the new Soviet offensive stopped this barbarous action. Warsaw did not existed any longer. 85% of city structure was in ruins. 50% of population dead. Except for that about 200 thousand of new-comers died as well. Those who survived returned to the city and began spontaneous rebuilding. This was later organised after the Capital Restoration Bureau had been established. Early success of this reconstruction has been hindered by the authorities who tried to adopt soviet experiments into Polish urban planning. Soon, the plan of restoration of historical Warsaw districts became a secondary question. The beginning of the fifties the work on restoration of considerable number of historic monuments stopped, while the remnants were demolished.

In January 1945 Warsaw was inhabited by about 162 thousand people living mostly in the undestroyed district of Praga (right side of Vistula). The number of citizens exceeded one million in 1956. Five years earlier the official borders were expanded so that the area within them tripled. The sixties brought a controversial politics of mass building from prefabricated elements. This substandard constructions spread in all suburbs and entered the central Warsaw as well. Huge empty areas in the city centre show nothing in common with a idea of a city centre and epitomise idleness and lack of imagination of the planners. Warsaw, now housing almost 2 million people, waits for a new developer who would match the pre-war mayor, Stefan Starzyński.

Mermaid statue at the Old Town City Walls

The Royal Castle ▶

The Royal Castle. Conference Room

The Royal Castle. Throne Room

The Royal Castle. Marble Room

Śląsko-Dąbrowski Bridge and the Royal Castle

Archidiocesan Basilica of St. John the Baptist

The Old Town Square, a view from Świętojańska street

Piwna street ▶

The Old Town Square as seen from the Cathedral Tower

"Pod Murzynkiem" House
◄ *Brzozowa Street*

A restaurant at the Old Town

The Old Town Square ▶

The Old Town. Barbican

Ul. Podwale

Uprising-Fighter Monument

The New Town Square and the Church of the Sisters of the Holy Sacrament ▶
The Old Town, seen from Vistula river ▶

The Virgin Mary Church
◀ *A view of the new Warsaw*

Krasiński Palace

The Monument to the Warriors of the Ghetto

Treasury Palace on Bankowy Square

The Opera Hause
◄ *The Blue Tower on Bankowy Square*

Warsaw Nike

Saint Ann's Church

Adam Mickiewicz Statue

Tomb of the Unknown Soldier

Saski Garden ▶

The Pałac Namiestnikowski Hall and Prince Józef Poniatowski monument

The Church of the Nuns of Visiting Sisters

Copernicus Monument in front of Staszic Palace

The Church of the Holy Cross

Plac Trzech Krzyży and Saint Alexander's Church

Downtawn

Marriott hotel

Mc Donald's

Holiday Inn hotel

Cricoland amusement park

Palace of the Culture and Science ▶

Ul. Nowy Świat

Sculpture at the Antoni Strzelecki house at Al. Ujazdowskie

The Ujazdowski Castle ▶

Łazienki Palace

Ballroom in the Łazienki Palace
◄ *The Monument of Fryderyk Chopin in Łazienki Park*

The Palace in Łazienki ►

Belvedere

Belvedere. Malinowa Chamber
◀ *Łazienki Park*

Królikarnia Palace

Wilanów. The Potocki Mausoleum

Wilanów. Detail

Wilanów. The Queen's Bedroom in the Mansion

Park in Wilanów

Wilanów. Front of the Mansion ▶
Chinese Arbor in Wilanów Park ▶